Word Weaving
A Guide to Storytelling

June 16, 1986

Dear Mrs. Sayers -

Now that this simple
little guide is in print,
I wish I could rewrite
it but... it *does* have
a freshness.

My best,

Kate Farrell

by Catharine Horne Farrell

Acknowledgements

The following people are the story behind the storytelling. My thanks to: the videotape storytellers whose tales are printed in this guide — Judith Coulter, first grade teacher, Jean Parker Elementary School, San Francisco Unified School District, who told "Elves and the Shoemaker"; Sharee Hunt, Cousin Wash's granddaughter, who helped tell "The Three Bears"; professional storytellers Robert Fish, Ph.D., who told the Sufi tale and Ruth Stotter who told the story about Anansi the spider; children's librarian Francisca Schneider who told of the maid Josefina; Cousin Wash (Curtis Hunt) who told a true-life story about the train, the Texas Special, which appears only on the videotape; Betty Morrow Bacon, University of California, Berkeley, who gave the manuscript a most expert reading and offered useful suggestions; Marjorie Fishman and Geoff Link at the Study Center, whose editing made this guide lively but precise; Mae Durham Roger who taught me storytelling in the first place and encouraged me all along the way.

@1983 Zellerbach Family Fund
Printed in the United States of America

ISBN: 0-936434-12-0

Library of Congress: 83-051222

Produced by San Francisco Study Center/Community Graphics
Illustrations by Leland Wong

Table of Contents

To the listener in each of us.

Storytelling: All-Purpose Art

N A TINY HOUSE IN THE North Countrie, far from any town or village, there lived not long ago a poor widow and her little son . . ."

Welcome to word weaving! This booklet is designed to help you on your way to an enjoyable lifetime of storytelling. It is a close companion to the videotape, *Word Weaving: The Art of Storytelling.* However, this booklet stands on its own as an all-purpose basic guide to storytelling for any occasion and any age group.

This guide expands the information given in the videotape and provides questions and exercises for further discussion and practice. In many cases, the guide quotes from the videotape verbatim. In fact, the text for the stories told on the videotape is printed here.

But the information in this guide is basic enough to adapt to any purpose. Though storytelling is of great educational value to children (see *Effects of Storytelling: An Ancient Art for Modern Classrooms*) and is easily done in a school (as the videotape *Word Weaving: The Art of Storytelling* demonstrates), it is as captivating an art anywhere: in a boardroom, at a dinner party, or on the commute train home.

Me?
A
Storyteller?

E ARE ALL A STORY, A LIFE story. We may see people's stories more clearly after they die, when we know how it all turned out. But stories are just as exciting in the middle of them, when we don't know what's going to happen—when we are living each day, page by page. It would be good to be able to share our stories with one another along the way. If only for the sheer entertainment of it, we might amuse each other with our predicaments and nonsense set aside in short stories, vignettes, anecdotes. But sometimes it's hard to know how to begin. So we keep mostly to ourselves and talk about the news, the weather, loose ends.

It doesn't occur to us that what happened just the night before might be interesting to anyone else. Maybe last night you were out grocery shopping with your three children and the St. Bernard in your compact car, and you ran out of gas on the way home. You and your kids and the dog piled out and had a race down the road to the gas station for a can of gas so you could be back on your way before the ice cream melted. You had so much fun running with them—after you thought you were so tired you could hardly move—that when you finally arrived home you ate more ice cream than you should have and went to bed early, tired and happy. Another page of your book lived out, untold.

Now some people seem to tell stories about themselves better than others. They're animated, amusing, entertaining and *so* believable. When you listen to them you're drawn right into the experience. Others tell jokes with such gusto that you hoot with laughter at the punchline. And still others can tell the plot of a horror movie they've just seen and set you on the edge of your seat, your throat dry. What enables one person to tell stories and events better than another, personality aside, is mainly the use of a few techniques that require some initial concentration. After you learn the basic dynamic that builds credibility, it becomes second nature. This is the art of storytelling.

This guide will give you the techniques of good storytelling you can use in any setting: office, luncheon, cocktail party, your child's bedtime, long car trips or at grandma's house.

Story material is as endless and varied as all the peoples in the world. Every person has a story; every culture has a story. Many have been written down from the oral traditions of folklore and legend, myth and saga. This story material weaves the universal fabric of all peoples' common experiences. The old tales have lasted through time. Each contains a truth spoken in story form or a satisfying story design that works well and fills listeners with delight. And they often are the best choices for beginning storytellers—they're easy to select from books collections. They're also removed from you, and you might not be quite so self-conscious in sharing them.

Children are the best beginning audience. If you already work with them, add storytelling to your program for their enjoyment and benefit. But don't limit your storytelling to the classroom or recreation hall. Use it at a staff meeting or at the next holiday meal with the whole family. Use it as a constant companion, warm, interesting and inviting. If you are practicing the true art of storytelling, people seldom tire of listening. They'll stop what they're doing and fix a certain fascinated gaze on your face until, of course, the story's over. Sharing yourself in stories might become a habit, and you'll never regret it.

Shaping and framing are the keys to telling your personal experiences as stories. Developing your own style is important, too, so you know how to tailor story structure and content to your delivery. If you have a slow and quiet style, you might work best with a few well-chosen details, and leave the rest to the listeners' imagination. If you are a bright, quick talker, you might use a lot of detail for a realy embellished and just as interesting tale.

The truth is that each of us is a storyteller already. We've all had many experiences; we all know the old stories intuitively, if not by heart. Most of us have felt no one would listen because we feel that what we've lived, or what we know, is neither interesting nor important. But just the opposite's true: What we can share with each other—a living experience through a story—is the most fascinating way we can communicate. Storytelling can become the thread that weaves through our lives and binds us all together.

Reflections

1. Think of someone who listened to you talk about the events of your life.

2. Think of someone who told you about the events of his or her life.

3. Think of a teacher—not necessarily a school teacher—who told stories.

4. Do you remember a special story from your childhood?

5. Recall the story from your childhood as well as you can: Think of how it begins, how it goes, how it ends.

6. Tell that story to a friend, to a child, aloud to yourself, or tape-record it and play it back.

7. Think of a story you know or one you've read that you strongly identify with. Find it and reread it carefully.

Seven Steps: The Basic Technique

ALL GUIDEBOOKS PROMISE to lead you from here to there. I want to take you along some well-worn steps, the well-traveled corridor of gypsies and minstrels, troubadours and shamen, and sometimes politicians and con men. After all, many practice the art of illusion-making, though you and I know that stories truly shared are told from the heart.

As I approach the steps of storytelling technique, I see seven. Not every practiced storyteller does; some may see eight or three or five or none. But when I prepare a story, I find myself taking these seven steps. I've thought about leaving out one or another, but I always come back to this same set of steps, the arrangement that works ideally for me. It's not a long, winding staircase, only seven straightforward stairs—the kind that might take you up the front porch any day of the week.

> ### Steps to Storytelling
>
> 1. Select a story you want to tell.
> 2. Learn the structure of that story and block it.
> 3. Visualize the setting for the story in your mind's eye.
> 4. Imagine the action of the story taking place as if you're watching a movie.
> 5. Read the story aloud, using your voice to project the images you've visualized.
> 6. Learn the story by heart.
> 7. Practice telling the story until it comes naturally.

Each of these steps is equally important. Perhaps they appear laborious, but after you've told your first few stories, you'll find yourself skipping up the staircase, hardly looking. You might leap over all seven in a single moment of perception or recognition. However, let's start at the beginning, as Dorothy did on the yellow brick road to Oz.

Find a Story You Enjoy

There are countless collections of folktales, usually found in the children's section in a public or school library under the heading "Folk and Fairy Tales." Such books are excellent sources for delightful tales and are easy to learn to tell, because they are gathered from oral traditional literature.

Modern tales, written by a single author, tend to have plot sequences that are difficult to remember. The modern stories might be "decorated" for effect and have a superficial or "trendy" quality. They also are likely to be copyrighted, so storytellers must be careful to give

credit to the author and respect the piece's style by
learning it word for word. Remaining true to the text can
be both difficult and restrictive. The old stories, on the
other hand, have been smoothed by retellings until only
the essentials remain. Though you often sense how these
timeless stories are going to turn out, you want to hear
them through to the end all the same.

As you search among the numerous sturdy folktales, find *one* that speaks to you personally, that you
consider especially charming, or unbelievably scary, or
wondrously exotic—a superlative tale, to your taste. Your
first story is going to be handled a lot, so if you
thoroughly enjoy the story material, you'll like the
learning process much more.

Learn and Block the Story

Read the story four or five times. Then draw its
structure any way you wish—boxes to show the scenes of
the story, an outline to list the story's parts, 3" x 5" cards
with each a separate section of the tale, a diagram or a
story map with arrows. Whatever form you use, you are
now determining the story's structure—its shape.

Here are some examples of breaking a story into
its constituent parts:

● "The Three Bears": two groups of three
parallel events with a grouping of three objects in each.

    1a. Goldilocks tastes all three porridge bowls
    2a. Goldilocks sits in all three chairs
    3a. Goldilocks lies down in all three beds

    1b. Each of the three bears tastes a porridge bowl
    2b. Each sits in a chair
    3c. Each goes to a bed

- *Millions of Cats* by Wanda Gag: a straightforward narrative of events held together by a refrain.

Cats here, cats there,
Cats and kittens everywhere,
Hundreds of cats, thousands of cats,
Millions and billions and trillions of cats.

- "Baba Yaga and the Little Girl With a Kind Heart":

1. Statement of the problem
2. Protagonist forced to confront problem
3. Protagonist receives tools for future use
4. Protagonist uses tools that match the difficulties exactly and therefore can overcome the difficulties
5. Solution of original problem

Put the structural work aside for the moment and re-read the story, this time noticing and perhaps jotting down the scenes or locations your story uses. If your story is "Hansel and Gretel," for example, you would have three basic settings: their father's cottage, the woods and the witch's gingerbread house.

Visualize the Setting

When you've identified the story's settings, close your eyes and imagine each location as if it were a movie set. Forget the plot and the people for a moment. Simply look around the story. Notice small details. See color and light. You are invisible on the set. All your senses function except your hearing. For now, the imaginary world of your story is silent.

This exercise calls upon your powers of concentration and may produce sketchy results at first. But stay with it. If you can see only a few specific details, try to sustain them as long as you can. Suppose you can see the outside of the witch's gingerbread house with its frosted-sugar windows and pink, blue and yellow icing. But when you open the door, everything goes dim. That's all right. Try to see one thing—the oven door, or the bed where Gretel sleeps—and leave it at that. With practice, you'll be able to open the door of the gingerbread house, walk in, pick up the herb jars on the mantel, sniff the brew in the pot, taste the jam on the kitchen shelf, notice the dust balls under the beds, feel the roughness of the bristles on the witch's broom.

Not yet allowing yourself to hear anything does hold your creativity in check. This is an artificial device, one I learned years ago from my storytelling teacher, Mae Durham Roger. Ruth Sawyer presents similar visualizing techniques in *The Way of the Storyteller* (Viking, 1942, pp. 142-144), though they're not original to her, either. Marie Shedlock considered storytelling a "miniature" with the "inward eye" being the "stage," (*The Art of the Story-Teller,* Appleton, 1915). For now, let's say that thinking of the story scenes as a silent movie set is a modern metaphor. The reason for silence will become apparent in the fifth step.

Now that you have a good mental picture of the setting, add the characters, going about their daily business. You see their mouths move as they talk, see them make facial and hand gestures, but you can't hear their words. Notice their clothes, the colors, the expression in their eyes. With this third step, you have built and populated the world of the story with your own imagination.

Imagine the Action

Now, run the silent movie of the full story. Begin with the first incident of the tale and let the story action roll. If you can't visualize the story from beginning to end, keep trying, go back to the text and start again. As you watch the story scenes move in exact sequence, get a feeling for which are fast-paced and which move slowly. Let the story build to its final and climactic scene, then let it wind down to the end. Switch off your mental movie projector and turn on the lights.

Read the Story Aloud

Using your voice is the most exciting and magical part of all. The reason you've been a silent witness to the story settings, characters and action is to keep your creative focus on the visual elements. Your voice now will provide all the sound the story will ever have. It's the story's sound track: You will do the descriptions, the narrative, the dialogue, sound effects and music (or emotional tone). Now, switch on the movie of your story again, reading the words aloud. Use your voice to project the images you are visualizing. Listen to your voice as you speak the dialogue, describe the settings, tell the action.

In good stories, the music of their words has rhythm and magic all their own. Let the story phrases roll off your tongue—as you do, relish the sounds of the words and the way they resound in you. Try these:

> Once there was and there
> was not a King of Spain
> who loved to laugh.

Cock-a-doodle-do! Turkish
Sultan, give me back my
diamond button.

Benjamin, my husband,
why are you standing
there in the street with
your mouth open?

Now read your story over a few times, refining the
expression of your voice to suit the words and reflect the
story's images.

A common alternative to seeing the story with the
eye of your imagination in order to learn it is to simply
read the story aloud over and over, or tape the story and
listen to the recording until you know the words well.
That way you allow the words themselves to weave a
spell, to evoke. Merely sounding out the words of a story
will call up in the listeners' minds their own images and
strike the chords of their own feelings.

Another way to internalize a storyline is to type it
out, slowly and carefully, seeing it form again into print
as if you were writing it yourself.

Learn the Story by Heart

Put the book aside. Speak the story directly from
your mental moving pictures. You already know the
visualized events in sequence, so the story is memorized.
You now know it by heart.

Tell the story to a tape recorder while it's fresh in
your mind. If you need to refresh your memory, play the
story back to yourself. Join in with your own voice, or
simply listen to the tape and use what you hear—your
own telling—to help clarify the visual story elements in
your imagination.

Practice the Story Until It Comes Naturally

The story now is ready to share. Practice on a child and then on a group of children, if you can—children are the least critical audience for storytelling. Next, share your story with a friend. And finally, try it for the occasion you had in mind when you first chose the story.

Reflections

1. Draw or write the structure of "The Three Bears."

2. In the structure of the story, highlight the climax, its culminating action, with a star.

3. Visualize the story of "The Three Bears." What are the dominant colors in that story? Why?

4. Describe the Three Bears' bowls in detail.

5. Describe Goldilocks in detail.

6. Speak the dialogue of the Three Bears when they return from their walk in the woods.

7. Tell the entire story of the Three Bears (see Page 45 for story text).

Style:
A
Personal
Craft

OU ALREADY MAY HAVE tried out or at least thought through the seven basic Word Weaving techniques for learning to tell a story. What you'll discover from here on, in your practice as a storyteller, will be your own. Storytelling is a personal craft. The Word Weaving approach is the one I use and teach, for it suits me. I enjoy preparing a story if I can jump into the story world with my inner eye, seeing each detail with a practiced clarity. However, this method of visualizing may not suit you. That doesn't mean you cannot become an evocative storyteller. It simply means you will do it your way.

There are many ways to render a story, from stylized gestures (as in the Polynesian *hula*) to dance (the "Swan Lake" ballet) to drum chant (American Indian) to simply using the power of the word. Whatever you find yourself spontaneously turning to *is* your way. You'll take in all the ways to learn and tell stories, and they'll combine and reinforce each other until you arrive at your own blend. Whatever method you've used to learn your story, at the moment you tell it your *personality* becomes the most prominent interpretive ingredient.

Storytelling is a one-man show. Like the Dixieland jazz artist who himself plays the drum, mouth harp and trombone, to name a few of the possible combinations, the storyteller takes all the parts in the story. Every character speaks through the teller's voice, every animal squawks or roars, every sun rises and sets in the telling of a tale. The tone of voice, facial expressions, hand gestures, body language express the story's emotions. All these are reflections of your personality as well, your unique style. The same story learned and told by five people often will be told in five different ways. As a storyteller, you'll discover your own style, and soon become comfortable and secure using it.

Have you ever heard a duck quack? The duck is making a definitive statement, easily, clearly and with resounding conviction. Ducks have an air of supreme self-confidence and don't seem to care at all that they often repeat themselves. That same simple, clear delivery is the best way to start telling stories.

It's often frightening at first, so if you can think of yourself standing your ground on two (webbed) feet and saying it all the way through, it might help. You may make mistakes, get tongue-twisted, even sputter and stop, but keep going to the end. This "ugly duckling" phase during which you may lack self-appreciation and self-image, eventually gives way to an elegant fowl of your own feather—you, a storyteller in your own right.

Begin by paying attention to your inclinations: Do you want to stand and have plenty of room for dramatic gestures? Do you want to sit in a big easy chair and invite people into an easy, intimate circle? Would you really rather be sitting on the floor? Move your hands to make a point? Take a moment in the story to pause and smile broadly, mischievously? Experiment with your own style, all the while concentrating on the story content. Expressions of your personality *and* the story should occur simultaneously and naturally.

You may find you like to stand quietly and tell the story straightforwardly, letting the story take center stage, your personality remaining a neutral backdrop. Or as you practice telling stories, you may feel a dramatic urge take hold and your arm suddenly stretches to the sky as one of your story characters prays to the sun god. Let these moments move you, take you into the dimensions of the story. You might discover something about yourself you hadn't known before or a part of you long forgotten. Let the story pull on you to find its expression, then follow your instincts.

Sometimes after a day of storytelling with different groups of school children I suddenly realize, "I feel strange! Off and on through the day I've been a monkey, a crocodile, a ghost, a little red hen, a mouse, a cat, the man in the moon. I stirred soup and swam rivers and scampered on the highest branches of the swamp trees." I'm not sure whether the characters have become me or I them, but we all enjoy the respite together. A close-knit relationship between teller and story is a sure sign your personality is playing its part in bringing the story to life.

Reflections

1. What are your two favorite colors? Why?

2. Your favorite outfit? Why?

3. If you could be anywhere in the world right now, where would you be?

4. List the five words that most accurately describe you.

5. What animals are you partial to? Which ones frighten you?

6. Recall a time when you were very happy. What were you like then? Describe yourself as a happy person in that story.

7. Enter a dark room such as a closet; close your eyes; listen to the sound of your voice. How does it make you feel? Accept your voice for what it is, and use it effectively.

Setting the Stage

STORIES NEED A STAGE, A certain framework in which they can be set aside, that marks their beginning and ending. The simple truth is that stories are made up of spoken words, ordinary speech, the same commodity we use when we order a new part for the washing machine. To signal that we now are going to "tell" and not "talk" takes some staging ability. Often that means looking for the right opening in a conversation, but sometimes "setting the stage" is more elaborate.

Imagine the face of a child at his sixth birthday party. Friends wearing birthday hats are standing around a table; the lights are off. Suddenly, the kitchen door opens and mother walks out, carrying a birthday cake sparkling with six bright candles. Everyone begins to sing, eyes fixed on the burning candles and the face of the birthday child. "Happy Birthday to you . . ." What child doesn't love the magic of ritual, eyes closed tight to make the birthday wish, then extinguishing the candles with a mighty whoosh? What child doesn't carefully wrap the baby tooth that wiggled out of his or her mouth and hide it under the pillow? What child doesn't mark those special holidays on a personal calendar like beacons?

Setting the stage for a story for children could become as extravagant as your imagination, and still be thoroughly enjoyed. A classroom teacher, for example, might buy a story hat to put on whenever he or she is going to tell a story. In some cultures, the itinerant storyteller was known by a certain hat, sometimes adorned with charms: Each charm was a story.

You could have a puppet introduce you and the story, or you might spread a magic carpet or rug where the children sit to hear the story. Perhaps you'll turn out the lights and light the story candle (a time-honored tradition), or ring a bell or chime to call attention to a special event: story hour. No child is going to think it's "hokey"—they'll get hooked on it. They'll offer suggestions, bring props or books from home, want to share their own stories, wear a costume from their wardrobe of old clothes. There's no limit to the appeal that "stage setting" has for children. When you have taken care to set a stage for yourself, you'll have their full attention. They'll hang on every word.

The outdoors offers wonderful possibilities for story settings. Perhaps under a spreading tree in the park, beside a granite cliff, or, best of all, around a campfire. Some settings, however, may look perfect but can present problems. The spreading tree in the park is wonderful until the power lawn mower shows up or the lawn sprinkling system is turned on or the neighborhood fire station responds to a two-alarm fire. Long hikes are a good time for chatting, but storytelling needs a body at rest, alert, and ready to listen. Still, some of the most memorable stories for children are told outdoors. Closer to earth, sky and animal, words ring deeply. Here, the circle of listeners around a fire at night needs no further staging. At a word the story leaps, full blown, out of the coals.

Holiday gatherings are times of ritual for children and adults. They are rich opportunities for storytelling, sharing common memories, reliving family histories. Perhaps after the big dinner has been eaten and all the dishes cleared, while the family is lounging in the living room, you might say, "Grandpa, do you remember the time way back when you first came to this country? And you didn't have a job or a roof over your head? Tell us about it. What happened? What did you do?"

Stories shared across generations are powerful messages. If you're a grandparent, your position in the family gives you the authority to tell the story of your life. Our cultural growth has accelerated so rapidly that a life incident 60 years past has an old-fashioned tinge to it, like a photograph from another era. The details of a grandparent's youth are truly historical now, so their stories have a kind of "weight of the ages" about them. Whatever story a grandparent or great-aunt or uncle tells is going to have an impact. If the older members don't know the prerogatives of their age, encourage them to perform this rite of passage: to tell the memorable stories of their lives to the younger members of the family. And as they tell, coach them. Ask for details, for their feelings at the time, for the lesson they learned from that experience.

Storytelling in an informal setting does need some direction so the group will know that Grandpa, for instance, is not just "talking" but "telling," and that something different from the usual after-dinner conversation is going on. The teller probably should try to catch the eye of everyone in the group and announce that he is about to tell a story. "Now do you all really want to hear about the long ship ride that took me around the southern tip of South America and brought me to this country back in '06, penniless and out of work? Well, if you do, just listen." Oldtime storytellers or just plain old-timers are famous for knowing how to "frame up" their stories and get you to listen.

Imagine this scenario: The old codger puffs on his well-worn pipe and leans back as far as he can in his rock-er. As he takes his pipe out of his mouth there seems to be a twinkle in his keen old eyes. He leans forward and says, "Now that reminds me of a story . . ." Even the cliche, "When I was your age . . ." might be the simple opener for an astonishing tale. Imagine your great-aunt sipping a glass of sherry and saying, "Crisp cool days like this always remind me of when I was a girl and the fall I got lost in the corn stalks and found my way to a small lake by the woods . . . I'll never forget what I saw there . . ."

It's true that the older you are, the more authority you automatically have as a storyteller. But don't wait for old age to creep into your bones before you begin telling your own stories. Telling them simply and unpretentiously in the context of your own daily life is enjoyable at any age.

Reflections

1. Think of a perfect opportunity to tell a story to a child you know well.

2. Think of a superb setting indoors or outdoors in which to tell a story to a group of children you know.

3. Think of a way to ask an older person, related or not, to tell a true-life story.

4. Think of a lavish storytelling ritual.

5. Think of a simple one.

6. Think of a way to make storytelling part of a family holiday or celebration.

7. Think of a way to make storytelling a part of classroom activity.

Telling Your Own Story

THINK OF YOURSELF FOR A moment as a *bon vivant,* a *raconteur,* a connoisseur savoring your own life. When you think about it, no one is going to fully enjoy your life except you; and no one will know why they should unless you tell them. No one in this culture is likely to ask you to tell them the story of your childhood, or reveal the most embarrassing moment of your life, or explain why, to this date, you get sick on clam chowder. Most people don't think such information is interesting. You'll find, however, if you are discreet, that telling your stories can make you a fascinating, authentic personality.

I remember that all through my young adult life I was embarrassed and humiliated by my childhood. I didn't want anyone to know where or how I was brought up; it seemed impoverished, backward. Later, as I began to meet successful people, some rich people, I found if I scratched the surface of their lives, I often discovered a background of poverty and struggle. The hard fact came home to me—most people are not born with silver spoons in their mouths. Over the years my shame has turned into a recognition and acceptance of everything that shaped and influenced me. They are simply part of who I am, and the story I make of it. Telling about my important people, places and events is a way of celebrating and savoring my life.

Whatever has happened in your life, you've survived, so in a certain way, every story in your life has had a happy ending—you're here to tell about it.

A compelling aspect of war stories—when people used to tell them regularly—was the relish of being the teller. A tragedy on the battlefront became an adventure in the telling. Your most miserable moments are worth telling because you've lived them. It can be like "singing the blues"—by the time you're singing them, you're on the way up. No one should think storytelling is only about the good times: It's about all the things worth remembering in your life.

Now what if you have lost track of your storyline? Where did it all start? Where is it going now? To get a sense of yourself and your own life story, take some time out to reflect. Find an island of time where you can be alone with your thoughts for an hour. Turn off distractions—no radio, television or tape recorders. Just listen to yourself. Let your mind ramble comfortably for a while, then try to remember back as far as you can.

Recall your first memory, not what your parents have told you, but what you recollect experiencing. Fix that memory. Try to visualize it and sense as much as you can about it. Concentrate on the details of people, setting, dress, furniture, smells, temperature. Summon tactile sensations: Were your socks itchy, your hands sweaty? Recall your emotions: What feelings did you have? What did you say? How did you feel about the other people who were there? Remember as much as you can, then relax, let go. Let the images fade and vanish. This is hard work, but an important beginning.

Replay your sense impressions of your "first memory" again. As you do, think of the beginning of the incident. What *was* the beginning? How would you start if you were going to tell it as a story? You probably would want to introduce it with a few details of place, time, your age, the others involved and their relationships. This gives your story a context, a setting and characters. Continue to the incident, the action. What was so vivid about it that made it worth remembering? Describe the incident in detail. How did it end?

Now comes the most interesting part: the conclusion. What does the story say about you, or what did you learn from the incident, or what did you learn about yourself in telling the story? There can be many conclusions: Draw one.

As you build a repertoire of true-life story material, make it a practice to set aside time to quietly reflect on the incidents of your life. The more accurately you remember information, the more vivid your story-telling will be. There's nothing like authentic detail: The listener can feel the truth of a chance detail all the way to the bone.

Use the following exercise to pinpoint *accurate* information:

1. Choose a year in your life, any year.

2. With the date in mind, gather whatever memory aids you have available: a photo album, old family correspondence, childhood toys, family history records, heirlooms from that time.

3. Close your eyes and recall images of that year. Let them flicker off and on at random, then look for important events of that year. Choose one incident.

4. Spend some time focusing on this incident. See it, feel it, use all your senses. Feel your emotions and physical sensations. Think your thoughts. Draw your conclusion.

5. Frame the sense impressions into the words of a story. Introduce the story, begin it, follow it through the action, end it and tell what it all means.

6. Jot down the story in your story journal. Use your own code or shorthand. Use sketches or other visual cues that will unlock your memory of this story.

7. Tell the story to a close friend. As you do, use your imagination to conjure up all the images, details, feelings and sensations that were part of the original event. "Tell" it, don't "talk" it. For "telling," the event must be well-lit with a freshness and immediacy, as if it were happening this moment. Remember the old opener, "I can remember it as if it were yesterday." Use it.

Now you've gathered all this story material, what will you do with it? First, you can realize that you are interesting. Your life is filled with color, feelings, drama, nuances, beauty, fear, dread, joy, misery and pain, as well as with special objects, favorite hats and worn-out teddy bears. And here you might have thought you were boring or didn't have any stories to tell! Next, you want to blend your stories naturally into everyday conversation. You don't want to bore everyone with your true-life stories. That's done by people who want everyone else to think they're interesting, but who don't think so themselves.

Suppose you're at lunch with a few friends, a time and place when most any topic can be discussed. Await a conversational opener for one of "your" stories: a key word, a parallel feeling, perhaps a chance remark. Train yourself to pounce on the opener. You might appear quizzical for a second and say, "Isn't that funny, I remember my father telling me something like that when I was a child. I had just come in the house covered with mud . . ." The most important point to remember now, once you've launched into your story, is this: *Turn on the lights, camera, action,* feel it, see it, place the characters and action in mid-air between yourself and your listeners. Don't talk about it, tell it. Live through it again. Then enjoy your companions' reactions.

As you practice the subtle art of conversational storytelling, use it for every occasion, business and social. If you can use a story to prove a point you'll be both entertaining and convincing. You might even begin to earn a reputation for being wise.

Reflections

1. Think of a way to teach a lesson on the seasons of the year by telling a story.

2. Think of a way to tell someone they just hurt your feelings by telling a story.

3. Think of a way to introduce a speech on fire hazards by telling a story.

4. Think of a way to ask a group of children to get along with one another by telling a story.

5. Think of the funniest story you ever heard. Jot it down. Tell it at the first opportunity.

6. Think of the saddest thing that ever happened to you. Find a safe way to tell that story.

7. Think of the most mysterious thing that ever happened to you, one you still can't figure out. Tell that story at an appropriate time. See if you find an answer.

The Formal Setting

O MATTER HOW AT EASE
you become as a conversational storyteller or how quickly
you win your colleagues' interest with a well-chosen
anecdote, you'll still feel awkward the first time you tell a
story formally. Everyone does. You may learn to enjoy
your moments in the spotlight, but not before you overcome the stage fright. After all, a storyteller is a one-man
show—everything depends on you. The story with all its
people and events must come to life through your voice
and inner responses. The art of storytelling itself puts you
on the spot.

Imagine this scene: It is open house night at
school; parents are visiting their children's classrooms,
talking with their teachers. The school bell rings to
announce the scheduled assembly for the evening.
Parents, children, teachers take their seats in the
auditorium. The principal announces a special treat, a
storytelling guest: you. You walk on stage, look at the

many upturned faces and clench your sweating hands. Except for a few creaky chairs, the auditorium is silent. What are you going to do? You seem unable to speak.

Let's leave you on the stage for a moment and discuss, first, what you are not going to do. Storytelling is not a dramatic recitation. A story told is at the same time easier and more difficult than a recitation. A dramatic recitation implies memorizing a piece verbatim and giving it "in character" (such as Hamlet's soliloquy), but storytelling demands that you recreate an entire living experience *as a credible narrator,* not as an actor. That means you have to establish a bond with the audience as someone both in the action as well as a commentator on the action. Therefore, you cannot lose yourself in the "theater" of the action, such as by extravagant gestures, props or elaborate costumes. Storytelling operates with the "power of delicate suggestion . . . this is hampered by the presence of *actual things*" (Shedlock, pp. 31-32). Storytelling shouldn't be stagey. Still, there is a simple solution. Let's return to you standing, sweating, on the stage.

The best way out of the fright and the only way into storytelling technique is to make personal contact with the audience. You are not an "act" or someone who is "in character;" you can and must establish a direct, natural rapport with the listeners. Look directly into someone's eyes and smile. Then look around the group, making eye contact, smiling. Feel how it feels to be standing in front of the group. Breathe easy. All this has taken only seconds.

To maintain a natural relationship between you and the audience and to give them some time to become accustomed to you, introduce your story with a few anecdotes. You might tell why you chose the story, its special meaning for you, its meaning for that night, or something about its cultural origin. You might tell a very short "throwaway" story that echoes something in the main story, simply to continue building rapport with your group. As you've probably guessed by now, the audience is an important element in the creative process of storytelling. They soon will become eye witnesses to your story. They need to warm up to it and to you so that when you do begin the story, your *personality* can fade away into the interpretive elements of the story itself. Pause.

Now it's time to begin. Give your story a title or identify it in some way, such as, "This is a tale of the Blackfoot people." Pause. Let your eyes sweep over the entire room. When you feel silence, anticipation, in the room, don't hesitate.

Tell the first sentence of your story in a clear voice; the first sentence frequently presents important clues to the rest of the story. Often folktales begin in the middle of the problem. Before you know it, the gazelle is talking to the beggar, or the cave on the side of the mountain is opening up for a band of 40 thieves. The beginning of a folktale (one from an *oral,* not a written, tradition) is like the banner headline on a newspaper's front page. That opening information is crucial: Now hear this!

Once you're through the first few passages and can start breathing again, remember to visualize. Click on your mental movie projector and begin to conjure up all the detailed images that make stories easy to remember and spontaneous to tell. Concentrate on setting, action, each character in turn, the appropriate tone for each character's dialogue. But don't worry, this is not an act, and there is no exact way to do it—there is only your way. If you miss a part of the story, leave it out. Try to fit that information in naturally at another point, if it's necessary to the plot. A few mistakes are part of this tradition. As with handblown glass or handwoven cloth, blemishes, personal touches, add to the value. Carry on.

When you come to the end of your tale, end it. Say nothing else. Pause. Wait for the applause; it will come. Again, greet the entire audience, smiling, using sweeping eye movements that include everyone. Bow. Leave the stage. The story has been told. There is no need to talk about the story after it is told—it has spoken for itself.

Imagine another storytelling scenario for yourself: A retirement dinner has been planned for one of the oldest and most respected members of your staff. You've been asked to put together some reminiscences about his early days on the job by interviewing other old-timers. You'll use what you gather to make an after-dinner presentation, taking the part of a pretend "eye witness" to the old stories. The first of the seven basic storytelling techniques—selection—has been done for you.

Gathering the juicy gossip certainly will provide amusing material, but your doubts start to surface immediately. Will I remember it all? Will I make each incident come to life so others will re-live the old memories? And will I appear a credible witness? Now use the other six steps to support you.

Be sure to group your stories so they build to some conclusion—either as examples of a certain character trait, or as incidents leading up to a finale, or some other way that makes sense to you. Then spend time reading through the story material, seeing each event take place with the eye of your imagination. Rehearse your stories to anyone who will listen: your children, your dog, anyone.

As the night of the dinner approaches, remember that even though you as the narrator will be slightly "in character" as one of the old-timers, you still will be the *narrator.* Create an identity for yourself. That night, find a way to introduce yourself that makes you accessible to everyone in the banquet room. The personal connection is the key that will make your stories work.

Try for a conversational tone that invites the listeners into the recollected experiences, almost an over-the-fence intimacy. You'll be surprised at the effect of a simple, low-key account of true-life events once you've established a natural rapport with the group. Everyone will feel that you are talking directly to them.

As you speak, keep your inward concentration on the visual images of each incident, as if you were remembering something that just happened the other day. Pause from time to time. Digress. Forget what you were saying, then remember. Repeat yourself. Be leisurely. The stronger the bond you create with your audience, the safer you'll feel to be the most effective storyteller of all: natural, authentic.

If you are a teacher, telling your first story in your classroom can be just as intimidating as the banquet hall. I remember having *no* confidence in my ability to hold the attention of a class with a simple story. No pictures, no movie or TV screens, no illustrations; a story seemed like a sure flop. I had chosen the English folktale "Cap O'Rushes," a 24-minute story that is a variation of the Cinderella tale.

As I watched each child take his or her seat, I thought, "They aren't interested in an old-fashioned folktale with kings and queens. They'll never listen to this . . ." Somehow I found my courage. I waited until I had the full attention of the group, introduced my story, looked around at everyone in the room, and began, "Well, there was once a rich man, and he had three daughters, and he wanted to see how much they loved him . . ." The class continued to listen as the story took hold and spun out into thin air. Then the story was over and they all had listened. I wish I had counted how many times after that they said, "Tell us 'Cap O'Rushes.' Tell us the story of 'Cap O'Rushes.' "

The warmth and intimacy of a small semi-circle of children is hard to beat. But not every storytime is as magical as my first telling of "Cap O'Rushes." Sometimes there are interruptions: a fire drill, a tardy student, a message from the office. Here are some tips that will keep the experience intact as you tell stories to children in any setting:

1. Find a quiet place for storytelling.

2. If possible, post a sign that keeps intruders out, "Storytime—Don't Disturb." Or perhaps post a student or aide near the door.

3. Create a special ritual for storytimes: a hat, a bell, a gong, a candle, to mark both the beginning and the ending.

4. Once the story has started, don't interrupt it. Do not stop telling the story to discipline or explain a word or answer questions. If the children are noisy, speak more softly. The tendency is to try to raise your voice over the group to hold its attention, but it will have just the opposite effect. Let them strain to hear you.

5. When the story is over, stop. Pause for spontaneous reaction from the group. Close the story hour.

Some of this framing, this formality, might seem artificial at first, but you soon will see, with experience, how important it is to create the optimum listening environment for a story. You already have given the story a great deal of concentration to be able to tell it—you don't want your efforts to be wasted on the desert air. Give the story an environment where it can thrive and be appreciated.

Stories, of course, provide rich material for language arts activities. When you tell a group a story for the first time, a formal setting is best. Frame the story so it can tell itself. Let the listeners simply hear it. After a while, tell the story again, informally. Use it as a reading story for retelling and listing vocabulary words. Act it out. Write it down. But let the first telling sink in undisturbed for what it is:

> A story, a story,
> Let it come, let it go.
>
> If it be sweet,
> If it be not sweet,
> Take some elsewhere,
> And let some
> Come back to me.

Traditional African sayings from *A Story, A Story,* told by Gail Haley (Atheneum, 1970)

Reflections

1. Imagine the storytelling costume that best expresses your personality.

2. What costume, if any, would you wear to tell the "Three Bears"?

3. Think of a formal setting for storytelling at a Scout meeting.

4. Imagine an adult audience for storytelling at a coffee house. How would you arrange the storytelling "theater"?

5. Think of a way to use a prop or two without detracting from the storytelling process.

6. Imagine a way to use puppets in your storytelling without drawing undue attention to the puppets.

7. Think of all your reasons for being afraid to tell a story, any story, in a formal setting. What is the worst that could happen? Name all your fears. Do you want to tell a story more than you fear to tell it? If so, your fears then become your companions.

What's at the End of the Rainbow?

ROM THE MOUTHS OF babes . . ." Everyone has heard a child make a startling remark that seems to cut through the muddle to some simple truth. Children have significant thoughts and feelings, and one easy way to elicit them is through stories.

Youngsters seem to work better with imagination and feelings than with literal description. Ask a child what he or she is doing right then, and I promise you the response will be, "Nothing." Ask a child what's at the end of the rainbow and you might get a better answer. Stories can be literal and imaginative at the same time, and are a way to bridge the gap between child and adult. We know that children love to listen to stories, but they also love to tell them.

The real test of a *bona fide* storyteller is whether the storyteller can swap stories with a group of children. In this game there is no ego, no position. You're only as good as your last story.

Try your luck. Get into a story swap game with a group of particularly imaginative children. As the game takes off, fast and furious, try to remember everything you've learned: openings, delivery, concentration, focus, and accurate detail recollection. But you may have to give up and enjoy a free flow of images and feelings, twists and turns of plot that defy every law of logic and physics. *That* is the living world of story-making.

Welcome!

The Elves and the Shoemaker

THERE WAS ONCE A shoemaker who made shoes and made them well. Yet luck was against him for, although he worked very hard, he became poorer and poorer until he had nothing left but enough leather for one pair of shoes.

That evening he cut out the leather for the last pair of shoes and then, after laying the pieces in a neat row on his workbench, he said his prayers and went peacefully to bed.

"I'll get up early in the morning," he thought. "Then I can finish the shoes and perhaps sell them."

But, when he arose, the pieces of cut leather were nowhere to be seen, and in their stead stood a pair of beautiful shoes all finished to the last seam, and sewn so

The appearance of elves or other magical creatures to lend a helping hand is a frequent theme in folklore. Their kindness always should be repaid. Traditionally, this story is told during the Christmas season and speaks of the spirit of giving. It is a quiet story with a tone of mystery; it can be told as if it is a secret you are sharing.

neatly, too, that there was neither a flaw nor a false stitch in them. The shoemaker was amazed and did not know what to make of it, but he picked up the shoes and set them out for sale. Soon a man came and bought the shoes. And because he was so pleased with their fine workmanship, he paid more than the usual price for them. With this money, the shoemaker was able to buy enough leather for two pairs of shoes.

As before, he cut out the leather for the next day's sewing, laid it on his workbench, and went to bed. In the morning, there again were the shoes, two pairs this time! The hammer, the knife, the awl, the wax and twine, the needles and pegs, still lay about on the workbench as if someone had been working there, but no one could be seen. The shoemaker didn't know how such a thing could happen, but he was glad it happened all the same. Again he was lucky enough to sell the shoes for more than the usual price, and this time he was able to buy enough leather for four pairs of shoes.

Well, so it went on. Night after night he cut out the leather and laid it on his workbench. And morning after morning there stood a row of handsome shoes, ready to sell, ready to wear. And day after day, shoppers came and bought the shoes for such good prices that the shoemaker was able to buy more and more leather and sell more and more shoes. At last he was no longer poor. In fact, he became a well-to-do man with enough money in his pockets to buy whatever he needed. Then one evening—it was not long before Christmas—the shoe-maker, after laying out the leather for many pairs of shoes, went to his wife and said, "What do you think if we stay up all night tonight, hiding? If we can, I want to watch and see who or what it is that is so good to us and comes every night to make the shoes."

"Yes," said his wife, "let us try to stay awake and see. I, too, would really like to find out who it is."

They lit a long candle and set it on a table, then hid behind the curtain that hung over the door. There they waited, struggling with sleep, until at last, just at midnight, came two stout little elves wearing ragged and tattered clothes that barely covered them. Barefooted themselves, the little creatures quickly sprang up on the workbench and began making shoes. They worked so swiftly and skillfully with little nimble fingers—piercing and punching and sewing, pegging and pounding—that the man and his wife could hardly believe their eyes.

And so the little elves worked on with tiny flying fingers, and didn't stop for a moment until all the shoes were finished down to the last stitch and peg. Then, in a twinkling, they leaped up and ran away. Next morning the woman said, "Husband, what I was going to say, those little elves have made us rich—so to show our thanks would be no more than right. They run around, poor little things, all bare and must surely freeze. Do you know what? I will make them some clothes and knit them each a pair of stockings. You can make them each a pair of little shoes."

Oh yes, the shoemaker would gladly do that. And so one evening, when everything was ready, they laid out their presents instead of the cut-out leather, then hid once more behind the door curtain and waited to see what the little creatures would do.

At midnight, there came the two little elves, skipping along, ready to sit down and work as usual. They looked, but saw no leather anywhere. They looked again and spied the row of little garments lying on the workbench: two little shirts and jerkins, two pairs of breeches, two peaked hats, four little stockings and four tiny shoes with pointed toes. At first they seemed puzzled, as though wondering what these things were for, but then, when they understood that the clothes were meant for them, they were filled with joy. Quickly they picked up one little garment after another, dressing themselves with lightning speed; and all the time they laughed with delight, and sang:

> Now we are smart gentlemen,
> Why should we ever work again?

When they were fully dressed, from peaky hats to pointy toes, they began to skip and run around like wild, so glad and gleeful were they. There seemed to be no end to their capers as they leaped over the chairs, and ran among the shelves and benches, but at last, after spinning round and round like tiny tops, they clasped hands and went dancing out of the door.

They never came back, but the shoemaker and his wife were always lucky after that, and they never forgot the two little elves who had helped them in their time of need.

Source: Based on the version of the German folktale from *More Tales from Grimm*, translated by Wanda Gag (Coward-McCann, 1947).

The Three Bears (Traditional)

ONCE UPON A TIME THERE were three bears and they lived together in a house of their own deep in the forest. There was a wee, tiny, little bear. And there was a middle-sized bear. And the other was a great, huge bear. And they each had a pot for their porridge. There was a little, tiny pot for the little, tiny bear. There was a medium-sized pot for the medium-sized bear. And there was a great, huge pot for the great, huge bear. And each of them had their own chair to sit in: a little chair for the little, small, wee bear, and a middle-sized chair for the middle-sized bear and a great, big chair for the great, big bear. And they all had their bed to sleep in: a little bed for the little, small, wee bear, a middle-sized bed for the middle-sized bear, and a great, big bed for the great, big bear.

One day, after they had made the porridge for

This is such a well-known story, with a clear structure and many repetitions of three. It is easy to learn, easy to tell. Have fun with it!

their breakfasts, and poured it into their porridge-pots, they walked out into the wood while their porridge was cooling, that they might not burn their mouths by beginning too soon to eat it. And while they were walking, a little girl named Goldilocks came to the house. She looked in at the window, and then she peeped in at the keyhole; and seeing nobody in the house, she lifted the latch. The door was not fastened, because the bears were good bears, who did nobody any harm, and never suspected that anybody would harm them. So Goldilocks opened the door, and went in; and well-pleased she was when she saw the porridge on the table. If she had been a good little girl, she would have waited till the bears came home, and then, perhaps, they would have asked her to breakfast; for they were good bears—a little rough or so, as the manner of bears is, but for all that very goodnatured and hospitable. But she set about helping herself.

So first she tasted the porridge of the great, huge bear, and that was too hot for her; and she said a bad word about that. And then she tasted the porridge of the middle bear, and that was too cold for her; and she said bad words about that too. And then she went to the porridge of the little, small, wee bear, and tasted that. She found it was neither too hot, nor too cold, but just right, and she liked it so well that she ate it all up; but the naughty girl said a bad word about the little porridgepot, because it did not hold enough for her.

Then Goldilocks sat down in the chair of the great, huge bear, and that was too hard for her. And then she sat down in the chair of the middle bear, and that was too soft for her. And then she sat down in the chair of the little, small, wee bear, and that was neither too hard, nor too soft, but just right. So she seated herself in it, and there she sat till the bottom of the chair came out, and down she came, plump on the ground. And the naughty girl said a wicked word about that, too.

Then Goldilocks went upstairs into the bed-chamber in which the three bears slept. At first she lay down upon the bed of the great, huge bear; but that was too high at the head for her. And next she lay down upon the bed of the middle bear; and that was too high at the foot for her. And then she lay down upon the bed of the little, small, wee bear; and that was neither too high at the head, nor at the foot, but just right. So she covered herself up comfortably, and lay there till she fell fast asleep.

By this time the three bears thought their porridge would be cool enough, so they came home to breakfast. Now Goldilocks had left the spoon of the great, huge bear standing in his porridge.

"Somebody has been at my porridge!" said the great, huge bear, in his great, rough, gruff voice. And when the middle bear looked at his, he saw the spoon was standing in it too. They were wooden spoons; if they had been silver ones, the naughty little girl would have put them in her pocket.

"Somebody has been at my porridge!" said the middle bear in his middle voice.

Then the little, small, wee bear looked at his, and there was the spoon in the porridge-pot, but the porridge was all gone.

"Somebody has been at my porridge, and has eaten it all up!" said the little, small, wee bear in his little, small, wee voice.

Upon this the three bears, seeing that someone had entered their house, and eaten up the little, small, wee bear's breakfast, began to look about them. Now

Goldilocks had not put the hard cushion straight when she rose from the chair of the great, huge bear.

"Somebody has been sitting in my chair!" said the great, huge bear in his great, rough, gruff voice.

And Goldilocks had squatted down the soft cushion of the middle bear.

"Somebody has been sitting in my chair!" said the middle bear, in his middle voice.

And you know what Goldilocks had done to the third chair. "Somebody has been sitting in my chair and has sat the bottom out of it!" said the little, small, wee bear in his little, small, wee voice.

Then the three bears thought it necessary that they should make further search; so they went upstairs into their bedchamber. Now Goldilocks had pulled the pillow of the great, huge bear out of its place.

"Somebody has been lying in my bed!" said the great, huge bear, in his great, rough, gruff voice.

And Goldilocks had pulled the bolster of the middle bear out of its place.

"Somebody has been lying in my bed!" said the middle bear, in his middle voice.

And when the little, small, wee bear came to look at his bed, there was the bolster in its place; and the pillow in its place upon the bolster; and upon the pillow was the little girl's head—which was not in its place, for she had no business there.

"Somebody has been lying in my bed—and here she is!" said the little, small wee bear, in his little, small, wee voice.

Goldilocks had heard in her sleep the great, rough, gruff voice of the great, huge bear, but she was so fast asleep that it was no more to her than the roaring of wind, or the rumbling of thunder. And then she heard the middle voice of the middle bear, but it was only as if she had heard someone speaking in a dream. But when she heard the little, small, wee voice of the little, small, wee bear, it was so sharp, and so shrill, that it awakened her at once. Up she started and when she saw the three bears on one side of the bed, she tumbled herself out at the other, and ran to the window. Now the window was open, because the three bears, like good, tidy bears as they were, always opened their bedchamber window when they got up in the morning. Out the little girl jumped; and whether she ran into the wood and was lost there, or found her way out of the wood, and was taken by the constable and sent to the House of Correction, I cannot tell. But the three bears never saw anything more of her.

Source: Based on the version of the English folktale from *English Fairy Tales*, collected and retold by Joseph Jacobs (Putnam, 1898).

The Three Bears (Jingle)

Once upon a time
In a nursery rhyme
There were (1, 2, 3)
Three bears!

They all went a-walkin'
In the deep woods a-talkin'
When along came a girl,
With (1, 2, 3) long, golden hair.

This is a modern adaptation of the old three bears, proving that the classic tales stay in the oral tradition and keep changing. Many rhyming versions, such as "The Three Soul Bears," exist, but not in print. The one given here is quite abbreviated. Try adding the missing sections yourself.

She knocked on the door
Ba-boom, ba-boom,
Boom, boom, boom,
But no one was there.

She went right in and
She had herself a ball,
Eatin' and sleepin' and
Rockin' and all.

She didn't care
No one was there.
She ate all the porridge
And she sat in the chair.

She went to sleep,
You know where.
....
....

Home came the three bears
Tired from the woods
Ready to sit down
To some home-cooked goods.

"Someone's been eating
My porridge," said
The Papa Bear, said the
Papa Bear.

"Someone's been eating
My porridge," said
The Mama Bear, said
The Mama Bear.

"Hey Mama, see there,
Someone has eaten
My porridge. Wah."

. . . .

. . . .

They went upstairs to
See what they could find.
And there was Goldilocks
Asleep all the time.

Goldilocks woke up and
She broke up the party
And she boogied right
Out of there.

"Bye, bye, bye, bye, bye," said
the Papa Bear.

"Bye, bye, bye, bye, bye,"
Said the Mama Bear.

"Hey Mama, see there,"
Said the wee, little bear,
"What kind of bear was
That there, huh?"

And so goes the story,
And so goes the story
Of the three little bears,
                Yeah!

Source: "White Horses and Whipporwills," Barbara Freeman and Connie Regan, the Folktellers, MTA Productions, Nashville, Tennessee, 1981. "Jazzy Three Bears" (traditional jingle) attributed to 5-year-old Shoshanna Korsakov of Chattanooga, who says she learned it at day care.

Three Jovial Huntsmen

There were three jovial huntsmen,
As I have heard men say,
And they would go a-hunting
Upon St. David's day.

And all the day they hunted,
Nothing did they find,
But a ship a ship
A-sailing, sailing with the wind.

The first said it was a ship,
The second he said, Nay,
The third said it was a house
With its chimney blown away.

In a quiet room, this rhyme can be spellbinding. It's a good way to still a noisy group.

And all the night they hunted,
Nothing did they find,
But the moon a-gliding,
A-gliding with the wind.

The first said it was the moon,
The second he said, Nay,
The third said it was a cheese
With half of it cut away.

And all the day they hunted,
Nothing did they find,
But a hedge hog in a bramble bush,
And that they left behind.

The first said it was a hedge hog,
The second he said, Nay,
And the third said it was a pin cushion
With the pins stuck in wrong way.

And all the night they hunted,
Nothing did they find,
But a hare in a turnip field,
And that they left behind.

There were three jovial huntsmen,
As I have heard men say,
And they would go a-hunting
Upon St. David's day.

Source: Mother Goose Rhymes.

A
Sufi
Tale

NE DAY, NASR-ED-DIN WAS
walking through the streets of the city, carrying a huge
tray of delicate glass. Suddenly, he tripped, and the entire
tray smashed onto the sidewalk, destroying every glass. A
large crowd gathered. Nasr-ed-Din stood there, then said:
     "What's the matter with you, you fools? Haven't
you ever seen an idiot before?"

---

*Nasr-ed-Din Hodja, a famous figure in the folktales of the Near East, is a rustic
teacher-priest of centuries past. He had a talent for being very foolish when he
did wise things and for being very wise when he did foolish things, as this tale
will demonstrate. Countless "Hodja" stories exist, many gathered in book
collections. Each tale has a punchline that, after you laugh, makes you scratch
your head (just for a moment) and think. This is a story of Nasr-ed-Din, from
the old Sufi Tales.*

Source: The Pleasantries of the Incredible Mulla Nasrudin, retold by Idries
Shah (Dutton, 1971).

Anansi the Spider, or How the Spider Got a Small Waist

ONG AGO, IN A COUNTRY called Africa, there lived first spider, and first spider's name was Kwaku Anansi. Now what Anansi liked to do best of all was to eat. He liked to eat just about everything. And one day, he heard there was to be a feast in Diabee. And then Anansi heard that there was to be a feast the same day in Kibbes.

Now at a feast you can eat as much as you want and Anansi didn't know which feast to go to. So he thought and thought and thought. And then he had an idea. He called his sons and he had them put a string around his middle and one went up to Diabee and one

This West African story is an example of a "pourquoi tale," one that explains how things came to be the way they are. Kwaku Anansi, the spider, is a delightful trickster character from the Ashanti people; he often is shrewd, but just as often is outsmarted by his own greed. Stories have many layers of meaning. This particular one teaches values without ever seeming to.

went to Kibbes. And he told them to pull on the string when the food was served.

Then Anansi waited and waited and at last he felt a pull on the string—up towards Diabee and he started out. But he hadn't gone very far when he felt a pull on the other direction—towards Kibbes. And both boys were pulling so hard on the string that Anansi was stuck right there in the middle.

Well, the boys waited until the food had been served and put away and then they came down to see what had happened to their father. But he didn't look the same. Where that string had gone around his center, his body was now divided into two body parts.

And that is the way all spiders have remained. If you don't believe me, you go look at a spider, and you'll see for yourself, that's how all spiders are to this very day.

Source: Based on the version of the African folktale from *The Hat-Shaking Dance,* collected by Harold Courlander (Harcourt, 1957).

Josefina

THIS WAS A MAID NAMED Josefina. She worked in a very rich house. This family was so rich that the milk they bought in the morning was not used up by nighttime. So whatever was left over, they gave it to Josefina. Josefina made very good use of this. She would take the milk to market every day and sell it.

One day they gave her more milk than ever. Josefina was dancing with joy on the way to the market. She would think of something and she would skip and jump. Her mind was far away. She did not remember that she

Counting your chickens before they hatch, dreaming of your trade on the way to market, doesn't always pay off. This familiar bit of folk wisdom is given here in a particularly Mexican version with Spanish words introduced throughout the story. Stories are one way to introduce a variety of cultures with their own ways of saying things (language) and their own customs. While children listen to a story line, they also can absorb a great deal of cultural as well as bilingual information.

was carrying the milk. This is what she was saying to herself:

"When I sell this *leche* (that's milk) I'll buy a nice big *gallina* (that's a hen) and that hen will give me *muchos muchos huevos* (many eggs) and I'll sell them quickly and with the money I get, I'll buy, you know what? *Uno puerco* (that's a pig) and I'll feed him acorn and barley and when he gets big and fat, I'll sell him and with the money I get, I'll buy *una vaca* (that's a cow), no, *dos vacas!* And what would those *vacas* give me? Milk, lots of milk. And what would I do with that milk? I'll take it to market and sell it. I will be selling the milk from my very own cows."

That thought excited her so much that she jumped higher than ever and, oh, she tripped. And she fell. And all her dreams came to nothing. There she sat, in the middle of the street, and she was saying:

"Adios gallinas, adios huevos, adios puerco, adios vacas, adios leche."

And to you I say, "Adios amigos."

Source: Based on the version of the Mexican folktale from *The Boy Who Could Do Anything,* collected and retold by Anita Brenner (Addison-Wesley, 1942).

Word Weaving Project and Materials

Word Weaving is a four-year-old storytelling program, funded by the Zellerbach Family Fund, that was developed and field-tested in San Francisco and Contra Costa County public schools. Its early focus was on training primary-grade teachers to become effective storytellers in their classrooms—they had access to workshops, classroom demonstrations and *Word Weaving: A Storytelling Workbook* (1980).

Teachers soon found that storytelling did more than enrich: It improved younsters' language skills and ability to compose and tell stories on their own. Word Weaving set about documenting the value of storytelling by collecting data from five classrooms in which stories were told regularly during a school year. The results were presented in *Effects of Storytelling: An Ancient Art for Modern Classrooms* (1982).

While the study was being conducted, a videotape was produced to help teachers and others grasp the techniques of storytelling. This year, storytelling is being integrated into the language arts program of the California State Department of Education, linking it to early reading instruction. Finally, this *Guide* shows how storytelling, a folk art that echoes ages past, again can become a natural form of human expression for all ages and any occasion.

For more information about Word Weaving: Catharine Farrell, Word Weaving: A Storytelling Project, California State Department of Education, 721 Capitol Mall, Sacramento, CA 95814, (916) 322-4981.

For information about Word Weaving materials: Word Weaving, P.O. Box 5646, San Francisco, CA 94101.

Effects of Storytelling: An Ancient Art for Modern Classrooms, by Catharine Horne Farrell and Denise Nessel. 28 pages, paper, 1982, $2.

"Word Weaving: The Art of Storytelling,"28 minutes, color video, available in ½" or ¾" format. Producer and director: Daniel Mangin, 1983.

Word Weaving: A Guide to Storytelling by Catharine Farrell. 60 pages, paper, 1983, $6.

Word Weaving: A Storytelling Workbook by Catharine Horne. This workbook now is out of print but is available at many public and university libraries throughout the country.